PAINTING PORTRAITS

How to capture likeness and personality

BY HELEN OLSEN

Photographs by George Olsen

GRAMERCY PUBLISHING COMPANY • NEW YORK

ACKNOWLEDGMENTS

The author and publisher wish to thank the museums and other collections designated in the captions for providing the paintings used for illustration; also M. Grumbacher and Company for pictures of brushes and palette knives; and Encyclopaedia Britannica Films Inc. for the copyrighted picture on page 59.

Arnold Mason's painting of "Susan and Dinah," daughters of Mr. and Mrs. Grenfell Bains.

Contents

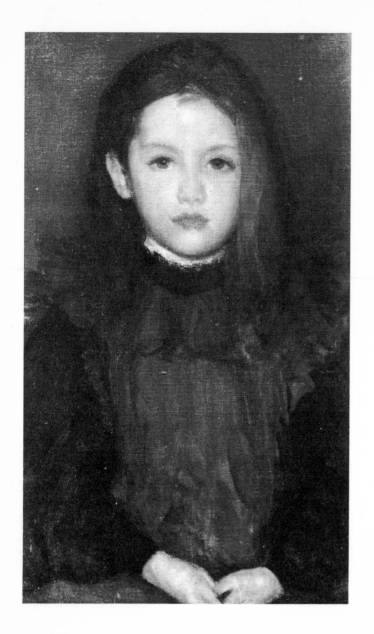

Whistler's "Little Rose of Lyme Regis" is a remarkable rendition of a head-on pose (Museum of Fine Arts, Boston).

Introduction

As eyes were made for seeing,
beauty is its own excuse for being.
                    —Emerson

One of the most rewarding experiences for any artist—professional or amateur—is to capture on canvas a living personality. Not only does the artist gain on the creative front, but he has the deep satisfaction of knowing that his subject can be enjoyed by his contemporaries and—perhaps more significantly—by posterity. How many of us know, and in a kind of intimate, personal way, historical personalities from their portraits! Think, for example, what a remote person George Washington would be if it were not for the sympathetic portraits done of him.

Portrait painting is a skill which, given the right enthusiasm, is not beyond the achievement of the amateur or "Sunday" painter. It is the hopeful aim of the author that this book will give would-be portraitists the necessary basic information to achieve their ambition.

The author feels strongly that, in addition to technical know-how, the painter must be sincerely interested in people. This, too, is a learnable skill, and one which the author will help you acquire. The first chapter of this book explains how closely related, in fact, are personality perception and painting techniques. The harder you work at your painting techniques the keener will become your perception of personality, and vice versa.

If you have a sincere desire to take up portrait painting, you will find it a most rewarding and enriching experience.

Modigliani's "Anna de Zborowska" (Museum of Modern
Art, New York—Lillie P. Bliss collection).

1.

Painting
and Personality

A portrait is successful when it reveals not only the likeness of the sitter, but the sitter's personality as well. In fact, a good portrait, regardless of style, seems to come alive only when it is imbued with the personality of the subject. Capturing the personality of a person is the highest goal of the portrait painter—and the most difficult to achieve.

Perhaps the most important quality one must have to capture personality is a sincere interest in people. If you have this quality, then you have nothing to worry about. If you haven't, then you can cultivate it, and what

Robert Lefévre's portrait of Pauline Bonaparte, detail (Wellington Museum, London).

Grant Wood's "American Gothic," a painting which typifies the image of the words *austere* and *severe* (Art Institute of Chicago—Friends of American Art Collection).

follows is the essence of my experience to help you achieve this.

When you look at your subject for the first time be aware of what his or her face expresses, and not whether it is handsome or beautiful. It is the quality of the face that counts and not its façade. If you want a practical example of the truth of this, then compare, say, one of the later Rembrandt portraits with a photograph of a beauty contest winner.

You can pinpoint the various characteristics of a subject's personality by putting your impressions into words; in fact, words can be a useful adjunct of the portrait painter. For example, when we describe a person as *prim* we tend to picture a lean-looking woman with lips and hands pressed together. Someone who is *prim* is often *austere*, even *severe*, a word which makes us think of a woman with hair pulled back tightly over the head. Grant Wood's painting, "American Gothic," typifies this image.

Detail of a Goya portrait of a *handsome* young woman (National Gallery, London).

9

Mysterious smile.
Drawing by George B.
Bridgman.

The word *mischievous*, on the other hand, makes us think of someone with bright, darting eyes in a fun-loving face.

When we describe a person as *glamorous*, we visualize a woman, well-groomed in sophisticated clothes and becoming make-up. The overall picture has a certain sparkling look . . . reminding us of theatrical personalities and movie celebrities. But add the word *sultry*, and the sight seen through the eye of the mind changes in a subtle but significant way. She now looks at us from under lowered lashes, suggesting *mystery*. The words *sultry* and *mysterious* usually suggest a brunette, although they could also be used to describe blondes, since it is the mood of mystery that comes through.

A *jovial* person is usually seen as smiling and *friendly*, with eyes that twinkle with mirth. Having viewed life from the lighter side, a *jovial* person is welcome at parties and social activities. His face expresses *warmth* in every line. This person may differ greatly, however, from the person we describe as *whimsical*, for this word may apply to the person who shows us the *whimsical* side of his personality when we least expect it . . . as with the person who may sit quietly during a conversation, and then with a single observation inject a note of *wit* and *gaiety*.

Words like *kittenish, gamine, elfin, pert* and *pixyish* all seem to connote people who are diminutive in size, but make up for it with a charm so attractive and appealing that we find their personality irresistible. We usually think of short hair, smaller features, and eyes that dance. Age in these types is unimportant, for this charm has no relation to the sands of time. However, the older person who can best be described by these words surely had the same unique attraction when young.

When we speak of a person as being *aloof, reticent, pensive, thoughtful, ascetic* or *sensitive*, we visualize a person who is a much more *calm* and less direct individual.

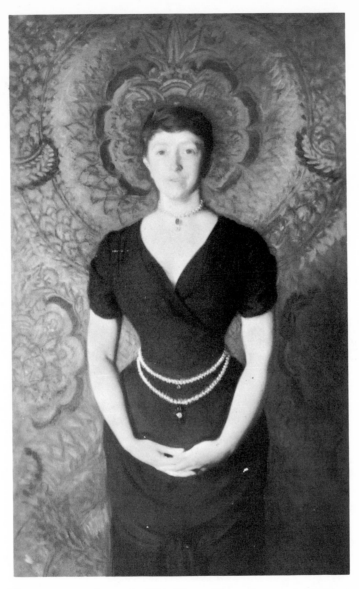

A *warm* person is seen in John Singer Sargent's portrait (portion) of Isabella Stewart Gardner (Isabella Stewart Gardner Museum, Boston).

Gentle, sensitive women are portrayed in "The Loge" by Mary Cassatt (National Gallery, Washington—Chester Dale Collection).

His gaze would probably not be directed at us. We think of this type of person as being tall, or elongated. Interesting examples of this are seen in the paintings of El Greco. He painted all his spiritual and religious figures in an elongated, even distorted manner, yet he painted his other portraits with normal proportions.

Although they may be different in their precise meaning, there are words which group together naturally, such as:

sympathetic, gentle, sensitive, and *warm*

A *pensive* young woman is shown in this detail of a portrait by Rogier van der Weyden (National Gallery, London).

. . . and others, such as
      witty, *fun-loving*, and *humorous*.
However, a person may be
      witty, *gentle*, and *sensitive*,
or . . .
      fun-loving, *humorous*, *warm*, and *sympathetic*.
People's personalities are changing combinations of elusive qualities. Sometimes the results of combining these words can be quite surprising. You may find several words which group together naturally, and one or two which seem directly opposite . . .
      pensive, serene, quiet, calm
          and
      MYSTERIOUS
         or
      QUIZZICAL!

13

This, obviously, would present a challenge to the portrait painter who had previously thought he had an easy, passive subject!

Sometimes you will find the paradoxical in your subject's personality. For example, a person's personality may be in complete contrast to the way she normally dresses. She could be

wholesome, sedate, poised, and reserved

and dress

flamboyantly!

Van Dyke's "Cornelis van der Geest" portrays a *poised* older man (National Gallery, London).

Manet made his "Woman with a Parrot" *whimsical*, partly through the setting (Metropolitan Museum of Art, New York—Gift of Erwin Davis, 1889).

Two aspects of the Duke of Wellington can be observed in these portraits. The painting by R. Home (left) makes him appear as a public figure of *stature*. Goya's portrait (right) seems to indicate a deeper and *suppressed* personality. (Both, National Gallery, London.)

An unexplainable paradox of words may suggest an inner conflict, or a suppressed personality, or any number of things, but it isn't necessary for the portrait painter to solve this mystery—only to choose which mood he wishes to paint.

"Tune in" to your subject's personality . . . and do it with a positive approach. You will notice that none of the words are unflattering, because nothing stifles creativity as much as a negative or critical attitude. Look for the stimulating, the inspiring, the humorous, and the basic dignity in every human being.

As I mentioned at the beginning, this method has been invaluable to me. I hope it is for you.

The next essential thing in the equipment of a portrait painter is an understanding of the architecture of the face. This is the subject of the next chapter.

2.

The Architecture
of
the Face

The gap between your mental image of the subject and the visual image you will create upon the canvas may seem great, but it grows narrower as soon as you begin to think in terms of individual features. By all means, keep your goal in mind—the complete portrait you hope to achieve—but meanwhile concentrate on one feature at a

Detail of an old woman's head by Velazquez (National Gallery, London).

Detail of an old man in a Rembrandt portrait (National Gallery, London).

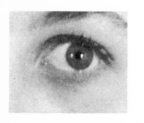

time, trying to analyze the part it plays in the total personality of the subject.

The Eyes

The four exposed parts of the eye are the pupil, the white of the eye, the iris and the cornea (see below). The transparent cornea fits over the eye like a watch crystal. The upper lid is like a stage curtain which rolls up and down, revealing or concealing the action from the gaze of the viewer. When the eyelid is raised, it leaves a wrinkle at the fold line. Observe it well, for it is a line which conveys much about the subject's age, feelings of the moment, and also some underlying personal attributes. Both eyelids have a certain amount of thickness, but the upper lid is thicker (and supports heavier lashes) than the lower lid. Note that you can see the inside edge of the lids from certain angles, as in photos 4, 5, 6 and 7.

Between the two eyes, when viewed from directly in front, there is a distance roughly equal to the width of one eye. This distance appears narrower when the head is turned to either side. The correct placement of an eye is far more important than the actual detailed drawing of it. It is the relationship to the other features that counts.

The expression of an eye depends to a large extent on a very simple phenomenon—how much of the iris shows! When a person is intense, enthusiastic and alert, he unconsciously raises his upper eyelids in order to see more. This causes the top eyelid to contract and more eye white and iris to show, making the eyes appear larger.

People who are shy and reticent are usually more concerned with their inner feelings than their surroundings. Consequently they tend to diminish their vision by what we call "lowering their eyes." Actually they lower merely the upper lids masking part of the iris.

The muscles surrounding the eye may also determine the expression. The corrugator muscles of the eyebrow

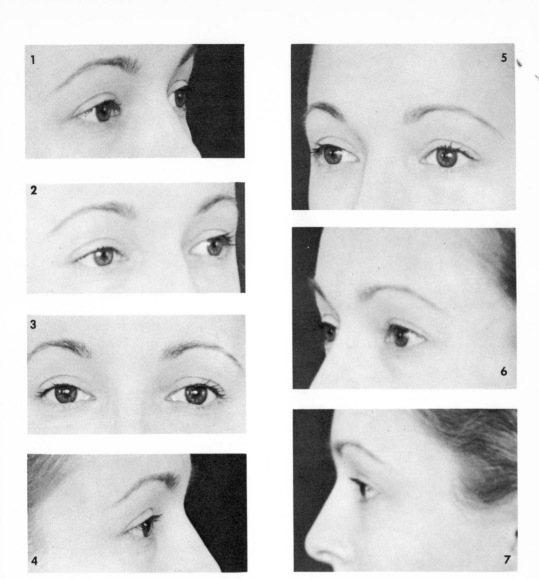

Note particularly the distance of the near eye from the bridge of the nose in photos 1, 2, 4 and 6—it is greater than you may realize. Photo 4 is not quite a full profile, and the distance is greater than in photo 7, which is. The full-face photo (3) shows that the distance between the eyes is almost exactly the width of an eye.

The wide-eyed, downward glance of the young woman in this detail of a Rubens' portrait shows how the eyebrows are raised in this pose (National Gallery, London).

are just above the inside corner of each eye. They press towards each other, allowing the brow to wrinkle and furrow. When a person is worried, concerned, angry, sceptical, petulant or quizzical he will be likely to press the corrugator muscles and furrow the brow. This motion causes the eyebrows to curve upward towards each other, forming a vertical crease in the middle.

In his quest for the true nature of the individual, Rembrandt painted many self-portraits, and chronicled for us his joys, sorrows and tribulations. In the portrait of an old face pictured here, study how the furrowed brow tells the anguish of a bankrupt and troubled man.

When we smile we press many of the muscles of the face upward towards the eyes. This pushes the lower eyelid upward, covering more of the lower part of the iris and elongating somewhat the outer corners of the eyes. A flashing smile, therefore, can be suggested by the eyes alone. Murillo shows us this in his famous

Detail of a Rembrandt portrait showing the powerful and complex architecture of an aged face (National Gallery, London).

"A Girl and Her Duenna" by Bartolomé Esteban Murillo (National Gallery, Washington—Widener Collection 1942).

painting of the two women above. In this detail from the painting, the duenna has the lower part of her face covered by her shawl, but a smile with gaiety and mischief is shown in the painting of the eyes and cheeks alone.

The Mouth

The mouth is the face's most mobile feature, but the lips depend upon the muscles surrounding the mouth for their expression. Studying the anatomy of these—or any—muscles will increase your understanding of how to paint.

We have seen how a smile can be evoked by the painting of eyes and upper cheek muscles without showing the mouth itself. When the lips alone turn up, we do not have a smile, but a grimace. A smile is an empty thing when the other features do not reflect it. To paint a sincere smile, the portrait painter must capture the expression of many features, but he must understand the action of muscles which control the position of the mouth as well.

The mouth is surrounded by a circular muscle called the *orbicularis oris*. There is a crease at its outer margin, sometimes called a "laugh line." Various facial muscles giving expression radiate from this muscle.

Drawing by the author.

"Portrait of a Young Man" (portion) by Botticelli (National Gallery, London).

This detail of Leonardo da Vinci's "Virgin of the Rocks" shows his genius for concentrating the essence of his subjects in the drawing of their mouths (National Gallery, London).

The upper lip has two planes, the lower lip three. These planes reflect highlights and determine the shadow pattern of the mouth (photo 5, opposite).

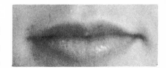

The mouth is not on a flat plane of the face, but goes around the circumference of a cylinder. Since the lips follow the curvature of the teeth, the corners are farther from you than the mid-point when the subject is facing you. No matter what the view, however, the mouth must always be painted in perspective. If the head is tilted

24

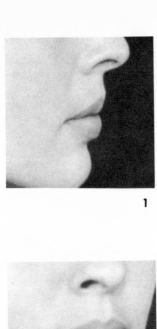

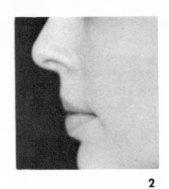

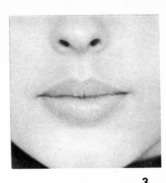

1

2

3

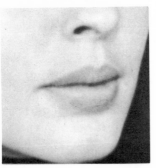

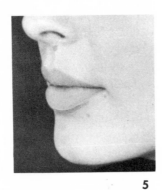

4

5

There are many planes of the mouth. Since the upper lip protrudes farther at its upper edge than its lower, this lip is usually shadowed, whereas the lower lip has an almost horizontal plane which reflects light from any source higher than the mouth itself.

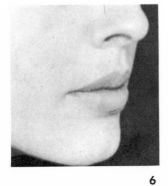

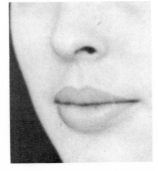

6

7

25

upward, the corners will be lower. If the head is tilted downward, the corners will be higher.

The important thing for you to remember as you paint your portrait is that the facial muscles will furnish the key to the expression. In an older subject, established wrinkles will follow the muscle patterns most often assumed, such as laugh wrinkle, frown or worry wrinkles, etc.

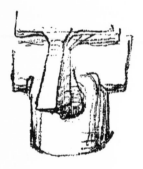

Planes of the face, as shown by Bridgman.

Drawing by the author.

The Nose

The nose itself does very little to determine the facial expression, but to the portrait painter it has an important function. The nose is the only feature which protrudes sufficiently from the face to create interesting and significant lights and shadows. We depend on the nose, therefore, for much of the contrast, design and form of our portrait.

The nose has four exposed surfaces, at least three of which can be seen from any angle. It is often compared to a wedge. It has its root at the forehead, its base at the upper lip. Two bone sections and five cartilages compose the nose. The septum originates at the upper lip and forms the tip of the nose. Flaring out on each side, two cartilages form the wings. The wings are raised in laughter and dilated with heavy breathing.

There are many types of noses, from the broad, flat Oriental nose to the thin, bony, predatory beak of the witch in Hansel and Gretel. The artist, however, is primarily concerned with the way light and shadow model the nose and give it form. The size of the nose should be considered mainly in relation to the other features. Its root and base both bear careful watching, for the nose may not run due north and south.

If the main light source is directed at the model from one side, the nose will cast a shadow on the opposite side

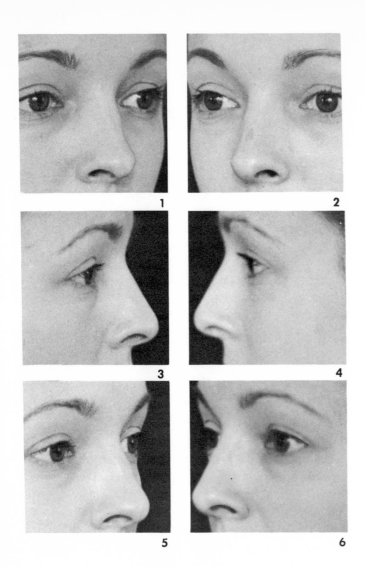

1 2

3 4

5 6

Use strong side lighting to accentuate a beautiful or distinctive nose, flatter lighting to minimize a nose.

of the face, as drawn above. This is an effect seen in many good portraits, and is a simple and standard way to light the subject. The higher the main source of light, the lower the shadow will be. However, even though the nose, lit from above, casts a strong shadow below it, the lower

27

plane of the nose may still be quite light. This is caused by the reflection of light from a surface below, such as clothing or a table, or even the lower part of the face itself. This same reflected light often causes an outline of light along the lower edge of the nose. Look for the effect of halation all along the nose by squinting at your subject with almost closed eyes. You will probably see this as a somewhat fuzzy line against the dark of the shadow thrown by the nose. Painting this halation will give your portrait an illusion of three dimensions.

Drawing by the author.

Notice that as the plane of the subject's face turns, an edge is formed which appears deeper in color. This is clearly visible on a black and white photograph, which tends to exaggerate contrasts (see above). If you look at your subject and squint, you will note that the edges of the planes in direct light appear warmer, sometimes redder, whereas the edges appear as shadow colors in the areas not in direct light.

Observing the bridge of the nose, notice that edges show on either side of the central bone. They both appear as shadows in a photograph, but if you make color notes as you look at the model, you will find that the edge of the bone in direct light is actually a very warm skin color.

The Ear

Certain criminologists have claimed that ears reveal many important facts about a person, but most people pay little heed to ears. We are aware of their presence, but seldom do we stop to observe them carefully. As a portrait painter you can no longer afford to ignore ears. Many lines of the face radiate to and from the ears, so that their proper placement is of the first importance.

Often the ear will not require careful drawing and delineation because of the view of the face. In a front view, for instance, the ears are barely noticeable unless

28

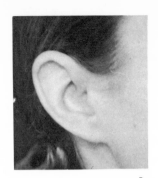

1

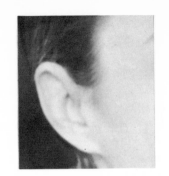

2

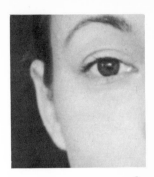

3

4

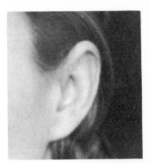

5

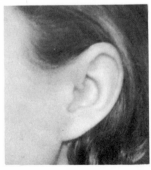

6

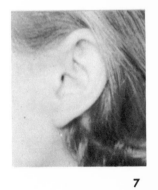

7

they protrude a great deal, as in the portrait of a small boy, but their placement must be right just the same. This also holds true for the portrait of a woman whose hair obscures most or all of her ears. The prominence of the ear increases as the head turns more towards a complete profile, if it is exposed to view.

The ear is made up entirely of cartilage. It resembles a shell with the rim turned forward to catch sound. Its planes are clear and the curlicues form an interesting design. The ear is lovely, delicate, and worthy of the painter's correct interpretation.

It is important to note the angle at which the ears are set on to the head—and the fact that the two ears often differ as to angle as well as shape. Light coming from behind the ear will render the thinner parts translucent, and you can express this in paint by making the shadows quite red. The thicker portions, and those not shadowed, will usually appear pink, even against a dark background with no light source in the rear.

All ears protrude somewhat, so that they cast shadows. The shadow of the ear is one of the most important in a portrait, and its correct placement will contribute a great deal to the viewer's impression of the subject's pose and attitude. It may tell a story of self-confidence, modesty or even timidity.

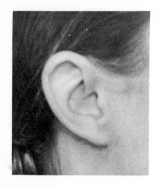

The three most important things to remember when painting the ear are its placement, highlights and shadows, and color. The modelling of the complicated inner curves should be suggested rather than stressed.

3.

Posing
and Composing

Most people are a little self-conscious when posing, but since you want the portrait to look relaxed and natural, it is up to you to put your subject at ease. The stiffness he exhibits will gradually disappear if you make a little light conversation with this purpose in mind.

Aim for a pose which your subject will be able to maintain comfortably. It should be casual but not undignified. Remember that a portrait is not a candid photo, catching a subject in a momentary position. A portrait that one can "live with" requires a certain amount of repose.

How Big?

One decision which should present no problem is how to scale your portrait. While there is nothing to prevent you from painting either larger or smaller than life, a life-sized head or head and shoulders looks best and is easiest to paint. You are unlikely to want to paint a full-length portrait—except, perhaps, of a child, but such a portrait would probably be less than life size.

A 14×18 inch canvas will be large enough for the portrait of a head and just part of the shoulders, while a 16×20 inch canvas will give you space for most of the shoulders. You can include more of the upper body on a 20×24 inch size, and one of 24×30 enables you to show one or both hands. A commissioned artist sets his fees according to the size of the canvas and the amount of

Cézanne's "Man in a Blue Cap (Uncle Dominique)" (Metropolitan Museum of Art, New York—Wolfe Fund, 1951; from Museum of Modern Art—Lillie P. Bliss Collection).

figure he includes in the portrait, but size must be appropriate for the picture. It is disturbing to the viewer if you crowd too much into your painting, but even more disturbing if you paint a lonely figure surrounded by too much picture space.

The size of the canvas and the amount to be shown have a great deal to do with the position of the subject. If you paint more than head and shoulders, avoid chopping the figure off at the waist or elbows. You can use a snapshot (see right) to good advantage in deciding just how much to show by masking the lower part of the photo with a sheet of blank paper until you find the most pleasing spot to "cut."

A helpful item is a small piece of stiff paper or cardboard with a rectangle cut out of the middle proportionate to the size of the canvas. You may hold this between you and your subject to help you determine how much to include in the painting.

The Angle of Head and Eyes

When you have decided on a general pose which suits the subject's personality and will form a nice painting, think about the angle of the head rather carefully. Some people tend to tilt their heads backwards or forwards self-consciously when posing. A head at an awkward angle may be appealing in a child, if it is characteristic of him, but it is difficult to bring off in an older person, and should generally be avoided unless you are aiming for a rather special atmosphere.

You may, however, wish to use a tilt to the head to bring out the subject's personality. For example, a head tilted backward can look arrogant, while a chin tilted down may look shy. Unless you wish to play up such an aspect, ask your subject to look at something which will cause him to hold his head in the position you consider best.

The angle of the eyes tells its own tale about the subject. If the model tends to avert his glance from you, paint him that way! If he watches your every move, you should paint him looking directly at you—and the viewer.

Eyes looking directly at you show a bolder, more direct personality. Eyes gazing off into the distance may look dreamy or ethereal and the pose is an easy one for the subject, who need not focus his eyes. It probably

Head back, eyes down.

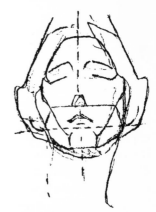

The head from below, as shown by Bridgman.

33

will be the best choice for the subject who asks, "Where do you want me to look?" Let him rest his eyes on a familiar object, gaze at a view out of a window, or perhaps an interesting picture.

No Grins, Please!

A big smile or an open mouth are usually very unsatisfactory in a portrait, no matter how attractive they may be in real life. People tend to tire more quickly of a grinning picture than one with a pleasant expression, and certainly such a pose is a tiring one for the model to maintain during sittings.

People smile with their whole faces, and you can show a sunny disposition without making the mouth the most important thing in the painting, if that is what you are trying to portray.

If your subject "does something with his mouth" such as thrusting out his lower lip, twisting his mouth slightly, etc., which is completely characteristic of him, you may want to paint him that way, unless the pose is disfiguring. In that event, try to get him to relax and think of something which will catch his interest and animate his face.

Shoulders and Hands

Shoulders turned slightly away from you look less stiff and uncompromising than when viewed head on. They need not both be completely in the picture, but this would depend upon the size of the canvas.

It takes knowledge and some experience to do justice to painting hands, and of course you need not include them at all. If you master this difficult task, however, the hands you paint will tell a lot about the personality of the subject.

You will find it very helpful to take a close-up photo of the hands in the position you want to paint them, for you may wish to work on them between sittings. The photo will also remind the subject, when he next poses, of the original hand position.

Folded hands. Drawing by Bridgman.

"Somerset Maugham" by Graham Sutherland, who once said, "The portrait is the most difficult genre in all art, for the painter is trying to extract the real personality of the sitter, and the sitter, nine times out of ten, is trying to withhold what he thinks one will get." (Tate Gallery, London.)

Portrait of Evelyn
Waugh by Henry
Lamb (Royal
Academy, London).

Personal Objects

If you pose your model holding an object that is dear
to him, you may accomplish more than you think. It is
comforting to a child, and gives the model of any age
"something to do with his hands." It adds interest to the
painting and may supply a needed touch of color or a
form to round out the composition. And it can contribute
additional insight into the character of the subject.

A book makes a nice prop for anyone who loves to
read. A man holding his pipe, though traditional, is
always interesting. A subject who wears glasses may
prefer to hold rather than wear them. Flowers or a toy or

"Peggy Bacon and Metaphysics" by Alexander Brook (University of Nebraska, Lincoln—F. M. Hall Collection).

Uninteresting
lighting.

other familiar objects are possibilities for a child. Unfamiliar objects, arbitrarily chosen, never look quite natural, and should be avoided.

The Artist's Point of View

Your viewpoint as a portrait painter should be level with or a little below the head of the subject unless you are striving for some very unusual effect. The professional artist usually seats his model on a platform. Another solution is to paint sitting down.

In painting a full view of a child or young person you might want to choose a different viewpoint—perhaps one looking down on the subject—but the orthodox view is best for a head or bust.

When you take preliminary snapshots (see below), remember to place your camera at the vantage point from which you will view the subject when you paint. The shutter of the camera should be where your eyes will be.

Lighting the Subject

The interplay of light and shadow on the face of the model is one of the most interesting aspects of portrait painting. The light shapes and models the features, shows the planes of the face and gives it depth and form. A complicated lighting effect, however, is neither necessary nor desirable. Some of the great painters of the past have used only the available natural light to create masterpieces of light and shadow. Who can forget the lovely light coming from a single window and falling on the face of a Vermeer? Or the sun-drenched faces in a Renoir portrait?

You can also obtain wonderful natural lighting effects with properly placed artificial lights. If you arrange them correctly you can place the all-important shadows exactly where you want them in your painting. The shadows cast by some features on others can alter the entire appearance

38

Renoir's "Girl with a Watering Can" (National Gallery, Washington—Chester Dale Collection).

Soft Lighting.

of a person's face, making him look younger or older, mysterious, severe, happy or sad.

It is best to locate the strongest source of light to one side of your subject's face so that it casts soft shadows on the other. You can use an ordinary lamp as a source of light, or a piece of photographic equipment. Of course, if you are lucky enough to possess a studio with north light—and while we are at it, we might as well choose the best: an overhead skylight—the lighting will take care of itself. Windows where sunlight can enter, however, are most unsatisfactory since the sun keeps moving and the shadows keep changing all through the day!

If you use artificial light, one source of light is not enough. Natural light filtered into the room through a window and reflected from light-colored walls may be enough supplementary light, or possibly an overhead light fixture will supplement a lamp or floodlight. If you find it necessary to use a flashlight attachment on your camera when taking a picture, try directing it to bounce off the ceiling rather than flashing it into the subject's face. A flash bulb photo will have only a limited use for you, however, as it will not be the same as the lighting you use during actual sittings.

Keep your lighting soft, natural-looking and uncomplicated and you will achieve a pleasing portrait.

Let Snapshots Share the Work

Have you ever wondered at the bored, blank, stiff or staring expression you frequently see in portraits? It's possible that the subject grew bored during the sitting! Unless you have tried it yourself, you may not realize how much effort modelling and even sitting takes. The ability to control and relax muscles at the same time is a truly professional achievement, beyond the compass of most people, and to maintain even a slight smile, say, for any length of time is difficult.

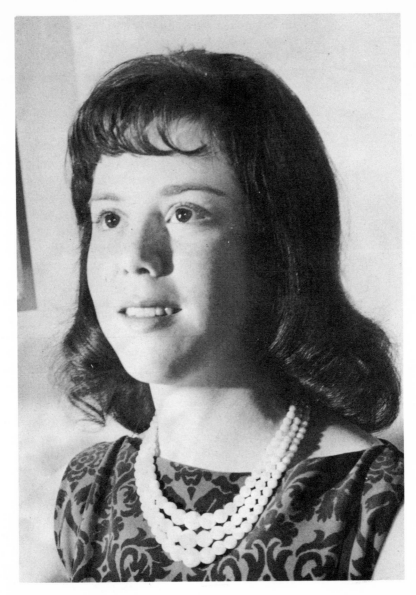

"Where shall I look?" The answer depends on the mood you want to capture. For steadiness of gaze, let the subject's eyes rest on a familiar object.

Time is another consideration for the sitter. Few people today can spare the time to pose the necessary number of hours a painter needs to complete a portrait. Even when a subject can give you a number of appointments, it is hard to work quickly enough to capture the freshness of an expression he cannot sustain for long periods.

Why not let snapshots help you solve this problem? A great many portrait painters, including the very finest, avail themselves of the benefits of photography, so you need not feel that it is beneath your dignity. In days of old, before the invention of cameras, there was no substitute for the living model, but nowadays there is no reason why you should not take advantage of the possibilities inherent in a snapshot or two. A few photos which capture fresh and natural expressions will cut down on the length and number of sittings necessary, and serve to refresh your memory of the subject as you work on the painting between sittings.

The snapshot does not replace the model and never will, but it serves you in the way that brief reference notes serve the extemporaneous speaker: to jog your memory of the subject when he is not present.

As for clothing, the photograph is almost indispensible, especially for the folds in clothing. For one thing, each time your model sits anew, even with one sitting, the folds will be different. For another, you want to concentrate on the model's face, not his clothing, during his sittings. This holds true for any background details you may wish to include, especially if you are painting the subject in his own home, office or any place other than your studio.

You will also find photographs of great help in working out your preliminary sketches without involving the subject. A photograph can never convey the glow of a complexion or the lustre and softness of hair as can a

Compare this photograph of a teenager, which catches the carefree youthfulness of the subject, with the picture on page 45.

model in the flesh, but it will certainly enable you to work out the correct placement of features, the changes you require for purposes of composition, etc., so that you can use every precious moment the model is sitting to best advantage.

Taking the Snapshot

Your subject may not be at all surprised that you intend to take his photograph, but it is possible that he may feel just a bit disappointed at the idea of starting out on the exciting project of having his portrait painted by merely sitting for a snapshot. You can tell him some of *your* reasons, but you may need to give no further explanations if you simply state that the snapshot is for *his* benefit— to enable him to assume the same position each time he sits for you.

It is possible to use a professional portrait if you are painting just a head, but actually an unretouched snapshot which you take is better for your purposes. The head of the subject should be large enough in the picture to enable you to see details clearly. Details of the eye, for instance, are very helpful for you to study, even though you do not intend to reproduce them photographically.

The lighting for your photograph should be exactly as it will be throughout the portrait painting, although you may find it necessary to intensify it in order to obtain a clear picture. Too dark a picture will obscure details. On the other hand over-exposing will wash out all character. A direct flash on the subject's face often has this result, and this is why it is better to bounce the flash off the ceiling.

The larger you make your photograph, the better it will serve you. If your snapshot is good but small, you might have it enlarged before you begin.

Three-quarters view from girl's left. View from right side was later chosen for portrait as it presented more of her personality.

44

The same teenager as on page 43, but the pose
creates an air of adulthood and sophistication.

Instant Results with a Polaroid

One of the best ways to obtain a suitable picture is with an instant-developing camera. Since you develop each picture on the spot in the camera, you learn in less than a minute whether your picture is satisfactory. Then you can immediately make corrections in lighting, position of the subject, expression, etc., as necessary. Continue taking pictures, correcting as you go, until you are pleased with the result. Don't forget to take a close-up shot of the hands if they are to be included in the final portrait.

The Subject's The Thing

Try to arrange in advance the setting you want to photograph. If you spend too much time fussing and rearranging, your model may get bored and appear tired and strained in the picture.

Remember when setting up for the photograph that it will only be a prop for your painting, so you need not be too fussy about unimportant details of the surrounding area. The person to be painted is the most important thing in the picture, and should occupy as much of the picture space as possible.

If you intend to paint a full background, including landscape, room interior or still life, it might be a good idea to take a picture concentrating on those details, without the model. That is an aspect of painting, but not actually portrait painting!

4.

Getting it down on Paper

Almost all artists start with preliminary sketches which they transfer to canvas. Once the planning is behind them, and most of the details and composition of the painting are sketched in, they feel the painting is 50% finished. After that they can concentrate on color.

Sketching and *re*sketching are always helpful, even if you are completely satisfied with your first sketch! If you

Detail of Degas' portrait of Manet.

spend enough time preparing and working on your sketches, you will become so thoroughly familiar with the face and features that the actual painting itself will run more smoothly and be more fun to do.

Before getting down to the techniques of drawing let us consider what materials to use.

Your Sketchbook

The sketchbook should be a most important item on your list of materials. It contains a permanent record of your ideas, impressions and progress. You should carry a small sketchbook with you at all times for quick notes and sketches, and keep larger ones for use in your studio.

The variety of sketchbooks in the artists' supply stores may bewilder you. An inexpensive newsprint sketchbook has the virtue of tempting you to use it freely and often. The enthusiastic painter will fill one up quickly! Usually the more expensive paper comes with fewer leaves per book, but you may enjoy the opportunity of experimenting with various types of paper.

Date your sketchbooks—you may even date individual sketches upon occasion—and save them! You will enjoy going through them more and more as the years go by. Then too, some day your sketches may serve as your only record of paintings you have sold!

Bulletin Board

Helpful, too, is a large bulletin board on the wall of your studio or painting area. Tack up sketches you want to mull over, pictures and clippings cut from magazines and newspapers that have a message for you, notes and hints and reminders of all sorts.

Sketching Materials

Pen, pencil and charcoal are most frequently used for sketching. Some people prefer a soft drawing pencil such as a 2B or 4B for quick or preliminary sketching. Others work with a charcoal stick, a very versatile medium.

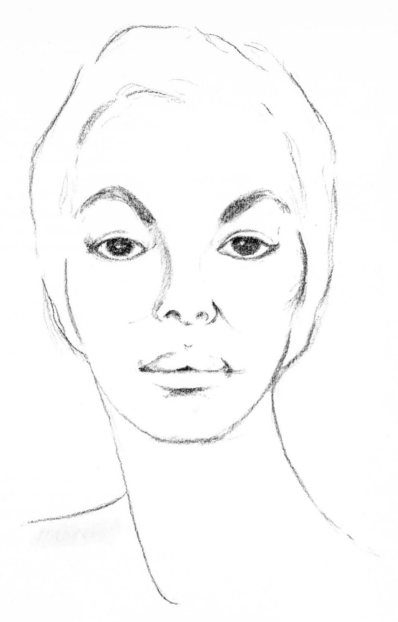

First sketch of girl on page 81.

Quick sketch with a
felt-tip pen.

A kneaded eraser is fine for making corrections, if necessary, in your charcoal drawings. Grey-toned charcoal paper adds another value to a charcoal drawing. It comes by the sheet or in a sketchbook and a white Conté crayon is useful for highlights on the toned paper.

Ball-point pens and fountain pens, while useful for quick on-the-scene sketches such as you might dash off in a train or waiting room, do not lend themselves very well to preliminary sketching for a portrait. Better is the felt-tipped pen which has gained wide popularity as a sketching tool. If you master the technique of such a pen you will find it capable of a wide range of darks and lights. Of course, you cannot easily make corrections and modifications in any sort of pen-and-ink drawing, though this need not concern you in a preliminary sketch.

Planning Your Approach

A systematic approach works well for almost all painting, but it is especially valuable in portrait painting. As a portraitist you will wish to take fewer liberties than the still life or landscape painter, who can change the placement of a tree or an apple as radically as he pleases during the painting process. An eye or a mouth, however, must retain its exact relationship to the other features.

You can make the first rough sketches either from life or from your snapshots. Which you do first—sketch or take photographs—depends on several factors. If your subject is a child, the snapshot will undoubtedly be your best starting point. It is difficult if not impossible to get a young child to hold a pose for even a few seconds. Often you will be unable to get the child to assume the pose you have in mind. You may have to take many different snapshots, and hope that one of them will capture the child in an agreeable pose. You may even have to combine parts of more than one snapshot into your working sketches. However, if you are a really fast sketcher and can catch

Durer's portrait of his wife, Agnes,
although only a pen sketch, cap-
tures form, character, even texture,
and is an especially strong design.

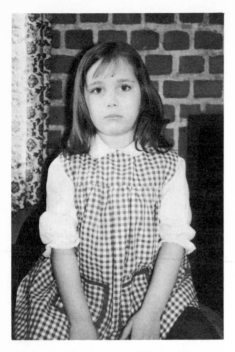

Stiff pose of a not too willing subject at a first sitting. (See page 4 for Whistler's treatment of a similar pose.)

Sketch drawn with charcoal on canvas after a suitable pose had been captured with the camera. (See color stages on pages 86-89.)

a pose from life, by all means try to do so, in addition to taking snapshots.

When your subject is adult you can expect complete cooperation, but here a second factor enters in—how much of the person you intend to include in the portrait. There is probably not much to choose from if your portrait is a head or bust. The more of the body you include, however, the more important composition becomes. You must consider not only the lines of the body itself, but whatever background you intend to include. Here sketching from life will be the happiest choice. Try your model in several poses, sketching rapidly but briefly, until you achieve good design and a composition which you feel will use the space of the canvas to best advantage. Snap the pose you decide on at the end of the sketching session.

Pencil working sketch in dynamic symmetry of a boy with a guitar. (See color stages on pages 90-93.)

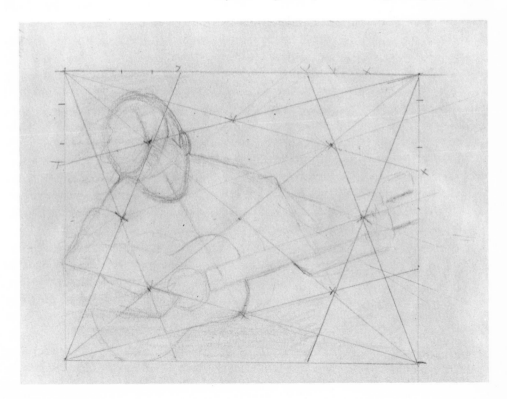

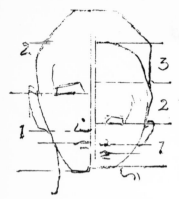

Comparative measurements of adult's and child's heads, from Bridgman.

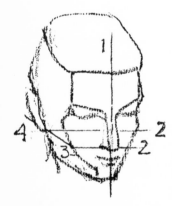

Construction of the head, as shown by Bridgman.

Form and Features

Sketching serves many ends. Good portraiture like any other form of painting requires a firm underpinning of good drawing. No matter how beautifully you apply the paint, how charmingly you choose your colors and how successfully you plan the composition, all will be wasted without good drawing.

As you sketch the head, keep in mind its basic oval shape. The eyes of an adult are just about midway between the top and bottom of the head. Though they may be the windows of the soul, you cannot draw them like the windows of a house. Notice that they are on a different plane from the rest of the face, canted downward below the boxy form of the forehead. Unless the model stares directly into the one and only source of light, the eyes will be lightly shadowed. Even the bridge, or root, of the nose is somewhat shadowed by the brow.

Anatomy is what we are really talking about now, and the more you know about anatomy the better will you be able to paint portraits. Nothing can supplant practice, lots of practice, in drawing from life, but a good book on anatomy will help a lot. (We recommend Bridgman's "Life Drawing," "Heads, Features and Faces," "Constructive Anatomy" and "Book of 100 Hands," all available in paperback editions.) Study and copy, study and copy and you will gain a feeling for drawing which will be invaluable.

Consider the nose. Note that its root is indented below the forehead. It follows, but does not necessarily parallel the contour of cheeks. Make sure you give it proper dimensional status. It is not a fin which protrudes from the face, but a three-dimensional form, regardless of how slender it may be.

See how the mouth follows the contour of the rounded face and jaws. No matter what the shape of the lips, the

54

mouth is not a flat, one-dimensional feature. Think of the jaw on a skull when you draw the mouth!

The angle from which you sketch the head will influence your drawing. Perhaps the easiest pose for you may be a full-face portrait, because the effect of perspective is minimized. The same holds true for a full profile, with no tilting of the head, but this is seldom chosen for a portrait. Perspective enters into the drawing, as you will realize if you think of the head as a cube. The effect of perspective is subtle, but you must give it some thought. At the beginning, you will be wise to choose poses which do not strain your ability to deal with extreme foreshortening, such as a head viewed from far below or above, or an arm extended directly towards you.

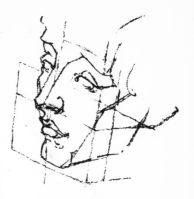

Masses of the head, from Bridgman.

Transferring Your Sketch to Canvas

Even though you are quite adept at transposing small-scaled and even thumb-nail sketches on to a large canvas, when it comes to portraits the job is exacting. You will find it extremely helpful to make your final sketch on a sheet of paper the same size as the stretched canvas. If your canvas is large, you may have to use wrapping paper, but if your sketch pad or drawing paper is larger than the size of the canvas, use a yardstick to outline an area the size of the painting-to-be. You will discover as you do preliminary sketching that each subsequent effort not only comes easier, but improves upon the previous sketches. This final sketch, drawn to canvas size, gives you one more opportunity to check and if necessary improve the relationship between the figure and the background.

By now, having completed your final sketch, you may be familiar enough with your subject to sketch freehand on to the canvas. Charcoal is a good medium to use, because you can easily dust it off with a cloth after establishing the form in oil paint thinned with turpentine.

Maurice Sterne's "Girl in Blue Chair" (Museum of Modern Art, New York—Gift of Sam A. Lewisohn).

Instead, you may prefer to sketch on to the canvas directly with a small brush and the same mixture of color thinned way down with turps. The sketch will dry quickly and you can start painting right away. A rag dampened with a little turpentine makes corrections easy at this stage.

If you are wary about resketching directly on to the canvas, there are several ways in which you can transfer your sketch accurately and easily. For one, you can buy a type of transfer paper which is available for this purpose. Place it between your sketch and the stretched canvas and secure both sheets to the edge of the frame with tape. Using the end of your paint brush, or any tool which will make an impression without tearing the paper, follow the lines of your drawing, adding all the details you wish to transfer, being careful not to move or slide the paper. When tracing is completed, remove the sketch and transfer paper, and the drawing will be reproduced on the canvas.

You can also create your own transferring devices from materials you have on hand. You can rub the entire reverse side of your sketch with a flat side of a soft drawing pencil, charcoal or a pastel crayon. Or you may rub powdered dry pigment on to the back of your sketch and then shake off the excess pigment. Tape the sketch around the edge of the canvas and make the impression as previously described.

These methods smear surprisingly little, and are all good ways to transfer the sketch to the canvas.

5.

The Tools for the Job

At this stage it is essential to consider the raw materials of portrait painting. Like all craftsmen, the portrait painter should take great pride in his materials. Although it is not necessary to possess every new aid that appears on the market, there are certain "tools of the trade" which make the task of the painter easier and more rewarding.

The Easel

There are two main types, the studio easel and the portable kind. Because of its larger, sturdier construction, the studio easel resists tipping and tilting and will hold your canvas securely. It is designed for indoor use.

The portable easel, which is primarily for outdoor use, is constructed like a tripod. Each leg has a separate adjustment so that you can use it on uneven ground. What it lacks in stability is compensated for in flexibility. If you have a studio, or a corner where you always paint and can leave your gear standing in readiness, the studio easel is the best choice. Otherwise, the portable easel will serve the purpose.

What You Will Paint On

Since prehistoric men first painted on the walls of their caves, people have painted on stone, wood, porcelain, tile, glass, fabrics, plaster, or almost any flat surface that came to hand. Most painters today work on stretched canvas.

A linen canvas stretched on a wooden stretcher frame

Frederic Taubes' "Portrait of a Painter"
© Encyclopaedia Britannica Films Inc.

is certainly the first choice for the portrait painter. Canvas board, which is really cotton canvas affixed to a cardboard backing, is not at all satisfactory. It will buckle and curl in a short time, and prove to be most disappointing.

Brushes

The selection and quantity of brushes is up to the individual painter. Clean brushes, of good quality, are a must. Each portrait painter has his own preference as to type. Some prefer stiff bristle brushes, some prefer soft sables, but most painters use both kinds, starting with bristles and finishing the details with sable. It is wise to experiment so that you may decide what is best for your style of painting.

By all means have a good selection of sizes and shapes. Round, flat and filbert shapes are all useful to the portrait painter. Wide brushes, one inch or more, are good for underpainting and covering large areas quickly. Avoid very small brushes as much as possible. They are too likely to tempt a portrait painter to paint endlessly and tediously and become involved with insignificant details.

Buy the best brushes you can afford. In the end you will find them an economy, not an extravagance! Keep them clean and flexible. Besides turpentine, there are many kinds of paint removers and brush conditioners. Old vases or jugs make good holders for your brushes.

Brushes—a selection.

Palette Knives

Palette knives were originally used for mixing paints on the palette, or cleaning paint off the palette for those painters who liked a clean palette at the beginning of each painting session. Nowadays they are widely used for painting, instead of, or in conjunction with, brushes. Knives are fully discussed in the chapter called "Painting a Portrait with a Palette Knife" on page 76.

60

A variety of palette knives.

Mediums

Some painters add a bit of medium to their paint as they work, especially if the oil paint has become too stiff or dry. If you use medium to dilute pigments, to paint an imprimature and to glaze with, you can buy it or mix it yourself. The ingredients are varnish, linseed oil and turpentine, all of highest quality. We find Copal painting medium, light, a good choice. Medium forms a bond between new paint and old when you paint over dried paint, and will prevent peeling and cracking in years to come. Retouch varnish will also serve to make a dry canvas easier to paint on.

Every painter needs lots of turpentine to remove paint from brushes and for general cleaning purposes. This need not be the best quality, but you will need grade rectified turpentine as a medium to thin your colors for underpainting if you use that technique. You can buy small metal cups to hold the painting medium and turpentine which will clip onto your palette.

Palettes

Like most painting materials, the palette you use is a highly personal affair. Even the way you use it is individual, and will affect the type you choose. If you hold the palette in your hand as you work, a light-weight palette of fine wood is easily the best choice. Wood provides a pleasant toned surface for mixing colors.

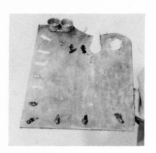

Type of palette that fits into a carrying case.

Modern palettes made of plastic and other compositions have appeared on the market. They are easy to clean and quite satisfactory if you like a white surface for mixing paints. Disposable paper palettes are handy occasionally and save you the trouble of cleaning up, but they do give you a rather makeshift feeling that is not too satisfactory for everyday use.

Many artists prefer to place their palette permanently on a table or high stool. It is far less tiring than holding a palette, and you can use a really large size—the larger the better! A slab of plate glass or smooth-grained marble, or a glass- or marble-topped table which you can devote to use permanently will work out beautifully. You can also use the smooth side of a piece of masonite.

As you use art supplies and materials you will find that certain kinds and brands suit you best, but regardless of the quality of your materials, they will be no better than the condition in which you keep them. Keeping your things clean and in order will make your painting hours happier and far more rewarding.

The Canvas

You can buy ready-made canvases or assemble and stretch your own. The stretcher frames come in sections, and you may keep a selection of various lengths on hand. You can then combine them at will into the desired size. The corners of each length are cleverly notched so that they fit together to form a frame over which to stretch the canvas.

Linen canvas is more expensive than cotton canvas, but it is a wise investment for the portrait painter. It has a lovely uneven texture which creates a very interesting effect and is preferable to a perfectly even finish and all-over pattern which form a rather dull background for the painting. Either linen or cotton canvas can be bought by the roll or by the yard. If you buy your canvas by the roll, the finished canvases should cost you only about half as much as the ready-made ones.

Preparing the Canvas

The more effort you put into the initial preparation for your painting, the more you will be rewarded by the final result. Stretching the canvas yourself, then priming and toning it, gives you a personal satisfaction you will not attain if you walk into a store and purchase one ready-made. Of course, bought canvasses are adequate, and handy when you are pressed for time, but your own canvas gives you a good, solid, "plus" feeling of achievement.

Assembling the Stretchers

We have already described the wooden stretchers which will form a framework for the canvas. They fit together firmly without benefit of nails or tacks, although if the corners are very snug, you may need a small hammer to tap them into place. After assembling the four pieces into a frame, square the corners by using a metal square made for this purpose. Another way to do this is to stand the frame, one corner at a time, in a doorway whose sill forms a perfect right angle with its jamb.

Next you insert the wooden wedges which come with the canvas stretchers, two to a corner in a sort of scissors formation in the slots of the stretchers. Tap them lightly into place with the hammer. The purpose of these wedges is two-fold. They will keep the stretcher frame from becoming lopsided while you fasten the canvas, and

The interlocking slots of the stretchers may slide together easily or you may have to work them in with a little back-and-forth effort and a tap of the hammer.

afterwards they will increase the tautness of the canvas when you drive them deeper into the corners.

Use a metal square to adjust each corner and recheck after all four sides are assembled.

Cutting the Canvas

You should cut the canvas material to the size and shape of your frame, allowing a 1″ overlap on each side. For example if the picture is 14″×18″ the cut canvas should be 16″×20″. Use a yardstick to mark off the desired size, pencil along the edge to draw a cutting line and cut with sharp scissors. Do not attempt to tear the canvas, or you will probably end up with a parallelogram instead of a rectangle!

Tacking on the Canvas

You can secure the canvas to the stretcher frame with either small tacks or staples. You will begin at the middle of each stretcher and work towards the corners. Start by placing the frame in the middle on the wrong (unsized) side of the canvas and tack an edge midway along one stretcher. Turn the frame to the mid-point directly opposite, pull the canvas taut and tack again. Tack the

Place the stretcher on the canvas while you cut, to keep the canvas from rolling up.

The original tacks will most likely be removed and replaced after the canvas has been pulled more taut.

other two sides in the same manner and then continue working towards the corners, placing the tack or staples an inch or so apart. Keep stretching the canvas and turning the frame as you work until you reach the corners on all four sides. Fold the canvas neatly over the corners and fasten.

Priming the Stretched Canvas

Your canvas, whether linen or cotton, is cloth which has been sized on one side. Even though you have been told that it is "ready to use", priming the canvas yourself by covering the surface with white lead is an important step prior to painting.

There are several advantages in working with a primed canvas. The rough, unprimed material will absorb a great deal of paint, causing you to mix much more paint than you anticipate each time. A painting on a surface which has been merely sized but not primed may look wonderful

The final tacks hold the folded corners neatly in place. A well-stretched canvas should be as tight as a drumhead and resound when you hit it with your palm.

as you work, but it is very disappointing to come back the following day and find your work has all "flatted" out through absorption of oil.

Too, the uneven surface (which may have its benefits in textural effects in some types of painting) will inhibit the blending of the paint on the canvas and interfere with the painting technique. All in all, you will save much time and effort in the long run by priming the canvas to begin with.

There are many preparations with which you can prime a canvas, and many painters develop their own particular formula. You can use flake white oil paint or buy a tube of undercoating, all prepared and ready for use. Less expensive and a bit more work is a combination of white lead and small amounts of finest quality rectified turps and medium. You can buy ordinary white lead, such as house painters use, but be sure to hammer the lid on tightly between uses.

Vermeer's masterpiece, "The Artist in His Studio" (Count
Czernin Collection).

Unless you plan to tone the canvas after it is primed, you can tone the white paint of the prime coat by mixing a little burnt umber with it. Burnt umber has the additional virtue of being a siccative (dryer) which will speed the drying of the paint. The prime coat must be completely dry before you can paint on top of it, and this will take several days, or even longer, depending on atmospheric conditions. Some painters prefer mixing a commercial siccative with the white paint to increase the drying speed, although others warn that the dryer may have bad future effects on the painting.

For the application of the undercoating you will find it fastest and easiest to spread it on the canvas with a palette knife, scraping and smoothing in the process. Do not put on the paint so thickly as to obscure the "tooth" of the canvas. If you prefer to apply the paint with a brush, choose your largest bristle brush and work it in thinly and uniformly.

Since it takes a while for a primed canvas to dry, you can see the wisdom of working up a supply of canvases, all primed and dry and ready to paint on. Some painters like to work on canvases of one or two particular sizes whenever possible, while others like to experiment with a variety of sizes and shapes. Of course, the commissioned portrait painter often has to paint to the size desired by his client.

A point you might bear in mind is the fact that standard sizes such as 12″ × 16″ or 16″ × 20″ can be fitted with standard ready-made frames. Unfinished frames are quite reasonable in price, and there are many ways in which the artist can personalize such a standard frame and harmonize it to the painting.

6.

The Qualities of Color

If we are really honest about it, most of us will admit that the real reason we paint is because we are completely fascinated with color. Learning more about color from a scientific standpoint will increase your understanding and enjoyment of color, and help you to use it to best advantage.

The Color Wheel

Most of us are familiar with the color wheel opposite page 72, but since it is the basis for all our understanding of color, it is important to refer to it.

The colors in our wheel follow a rainbow pattern. The three basic colors—the primary colors—are red, yellow and blue. All the other colors can be mixed from these three. They are equidistant from each other on the color wheel, forming a triangle. The secondary colors are green, a mixture of blue and yellow; orange, a mixture of yellow and red; and violet, a mixture of red and blue.

Colors directly opposite each other on the wheel are called complementary colors. They complement or complete each other, adding up to the three primary colors. For instance, the complementary colors red and green could be expressed as red and blue-plus-yellow.

When two complementary colors are mixed equally they form a neutral grey, not a particularly desirable color in painting. If you mix them in unequal amounts, however, the greying or toning effect can be a very nice one.

You can make a brown by mixing one part of a primary color and two parts of its complementary color. Black and white are technically not colors and consequently are not found on the color wheel.

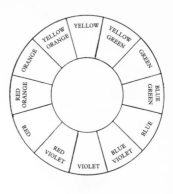

Warm and Cool Colors

If the color wheel were divided in half longitudinally, the right side would consist of "warm" colors and the left side "cool". We think of reds, oranges and yellows as being warm, and associate them with sunlight, fire and heat. We think of blues and greens as cool, since they remind us of water, grass and trees.

Warm colors seem to come towards us, while cool colors recede. This is true in nature as well as on canvas. Distant hills look blue and, as they recede, even a cool purple. Even the green of a sunny meadow, full of warm yellow in the foreground, grows bluish in the distance. These are facts which the observant landscape painter deals with constantly, but the portraitist can take advantage of them too. After all, his problem of making a nose or forehead, cheekbones or chin come forward, while eye-sockets and other hollows recede, is not so very different.

Setting Up the Palette

Just as the organization of color into a color wheel helps our understanding of color, organizing the palette similarly facilitates the use of color.

Begin by placing the three earth colors, black, burnt umber and burnt sienna in the short space next to the thumb hole of the palette—or on the right side of a palette with no hole. Turning the corner and going from right to left across the top, place the warm colors, beginning with yellow. The colors you put out will vary according to the painting, but you might place yellow ochre next, cadmium yellow, Venetian followed by cadmium red, and then alizarin crimson. If you use manganese violet, it would go at the upper left-hand corner. Running down the left side are the cool colors—ultramarine, Prussian or cobalt blue and finally viridian green. White goes in the remaining corner, the lower right. This arrangement leaves one side as well as the middle of the palette free for mixing. You may add other colors in order as you wish.

A Color System

As the science of color developed, a few color experts recognized the need for some general ground rules concerning color. The system widely in use today is called the Munsel system. It is based on the theory that there are three constant properties of color: hue, value and intensity.

Hue refers strictly to the name of the color, such as red, green or orange. Value means lightness or darkness. It has been proven that the human eye can distinguish between ten shades, ranging within a given hue.

Contrast and Harmony

Perhaps one of the most important elements to consider in the use of color is contrast. Fundamentally, contrast means only difference, but it can mean much more to the artist. It can mean variety of lights and darks in a painting, keeping it from being monotonous. It can mean difference in texture, as when the thick areas of paint contrast with the interesting pattern of the canvas showing through the thinner layers. Smooth blended areas of paint may contrast with the ridges and furrows made by a knife or bristle brush. Warm colors are contrasted with cool colors. Bright colors look much brighter when placed next to greyer colors. Contrast adds interest to painting.

There are no set rules for determining color harmony, although a great many people have tried to work out formulas or systems. Your own taste will always be the guiding factor, but your taste will change often. Experi-

ment wildly and freely, attempting everything and fearing nothing! Spread paint over your palette, combine colors, juxtapose darks and lights, grey and pure colors, hues and tones!

There are no "do's" or "don'ts" when it comes to color, but there are a few facts to bear in mind. For instance, when you use large amounts of one color it is always good to introduce the complementary color in order to rest the eye of the viewer. You can understand this if you stare hard at a bright color for a minute or so, and then close your eyes, or gaze at a blank sheet of white paper. The exact complementary color will appear! Something about the chemistry of the eye or of the brain, causes this to happen, but you facilitate the process by adding a dash of red to a field of green, or some blue shadows in the folds of a yellow cloth.

Greying your colors is another important factor in creating a telling sense of harmony. Using colors of similar intensity, or similar values leads to a static state of affairs. Even the brightest, sharpest colors negate each other in time. In nature we see that the bright colors of flowers are harmonious because of the duller greens of the foliage—although in early spring, the bright greens of young foliage may contrast and harmonize with the dull earth colors of bark and branch!

Unity Through Color

A painting has unity if all areas are related. One way to achieve unity through color is by the use of repetition. One good dash of blue deserves another! Each spot or area of color will enhance the other, for the eye of the viewer tends to follow first one color, then another, around the plane of the picture. This is not a conscious act, but it happens just the same, and that is why it is bad to have some one color appear only once. It will stop the roving eye like a stop-light. Repeated colors attract the eye, and perhaps the "inner eye" of the beholder, from place to place, correlating and unifying the picture for him.

Working with black and white in addition to only one other color, or perhaps just two other colors, is an interesting experiment to perform. It will teach you a great deal about many aspects of color in general, and the specific properties of your one or two colors in particular, and at the same time, you can create a very unusual and effective painting or portrait.

Mixing Fresh Colors

Since all colors are based on primary colors, it follows that you can mix any flesh tones from a palette containing just the three primary colors. It is rather theoretical, however, and not a practice to be recommended. Here are some particularly nice combinations for flesh colors which you will enjoy experimenting with:

Yellow ochre; *cadmium red, light*; *viridian green*, plus white. In the warm flesh areas, the viridian is added in small amounts to grey the warm colors and slightly reduce their intensity. More green is used in the cooler shadowed areas.

Yellow ochre; *cadmium red, light*; *ivory black*, plus white. Black is used in this combination in the same manner as green in the first example to tone the warm areas and create a shadow color. Black mixed with cadmium red and very little white makes a suitable color for painting eyebrows and the darker areas of the eyes, as well as the nostrils of the nose. With the addition of more white, it becomes a lovely violet-brown shadow color. Do not be afraid to use limited amounts of black in mixing with other colors. It is a dead color only when used alone.

Another fine variation is to replace the black in the above combination with burnt umber. The addition of smaller or larger amounts of the umber gives this mixture a very wide scope of flesh tones, from fair to dark skin.

Yellow ochre; *Venetian red*; *ultramarine blue*, plus white. Venetian red is a reddish brown color of great intensity which requires careful mixing because a little goes a long way. Mixed with white, it makes a lovely soft pink. It is very harmonious with yellow ochre, and ultramarine blue is a fine color for further toning the mixture and creating shadow colors.

Local Color and Reflected Light

When we speak of local color we refer to the appearance of the object in normal light. The local color of a lemon is yellow. If, however, the lemon is placed on a green tablecloth in front of a window with strong light, the tablecloth will reflect on the lower part of the lemon, causing it to appear green. The local color of the lemon is still yellow, but in this case the reflected light is green.

As we look at our subject, we must determine which colors are local and which are reflected light, a task that may not be simple. There may be obvious reflections from clothing or a nearby object on the flesh of a sitter, but reflections can be quite subtle in the shadowed areas.

Reflected light may add either warmth or coolness to the flesh tones. When the influence occurs in the shadows, a careful analysis will help you decide which color to choose to darken or grey those portions. The actual color of reflected light on the high spots—such as forehead, cheekbones or chin—is more straightforward and easier to determine.

The shadow cast by an object is the complement of the object's local color. For example, if we place our lemon on a neutral surface, the shadow it casts on that surface will have a violet cast, since violet is the complementary color of yellow. The same reaction occurs on flesh colors. If your subject has a very pink or ruddy complexion, the shadows cast by some features on others will have a greenish tinge. A subject with golden or blonde coloring will have shadows with a violet cast.

7.

Painting a Portrait with a Palette Knife

Palette knives have come a long way since they were used only for mixing the color pigments on the palette! The original palette knife had a long flat blade projecting straight from the handle to a rounded end. Such knives are still available and are handy for use on the palette— even when you are painting with a brush.

For knife painting, however, newer types of knives allow you to use both blade and edge more freely. The blade is angled to the handle in the manner of a trowel, so that the handle does not interfere with the use of the blade. The shoulder in the shank allows you to apply paint to the canvas without dragging your knuckles across wet paint.

In shape most knife blades today are modified triangles, long or short, fat or thin, rounded or pointed. Some are very small and used for detail work, and others have blades of six inches or more. The large trowel-shaped knives can cover big areas quickly and are useful when working on very big canvases.

Knife Painting Techniques

There are as many different ways to use a palette knife as a brush, and it is a versatile tool which lends itself to experimentation. Even a small selection of knives will give you ample scope to try the techniques which follow and you will enjoy the many new discoveries you are bound to develop on your own.

You can lay color thickly on to your painting by using the knife as a trowel. This gives the paint a highly textured or sculptured effect. You can scrape color thinly on to the canvas. You can scrape one color thinly over another. Or you can scrape and blend one color into another on the canvas.

You can put color on thickly and then scrape it off, leaving a residue of pigment and creating misty, ethereal effects. The palette knife allows you to "reach through" wet paint to pick up or expose a color underneath, perhaps from the underpainting.

You can blend colors on the canvas itself as well as on the palette. For instance, you can stipple it on with the flat of the blade, creating a slight textural effect, or you can mix it more thoroughly by "puddling" two colors together. You can smooth over the paint with a broad-bladed knife if you want a smooth surface. You can pick up colors with the edge of the knife (from the palette) and spread them across an area already painted. To create a "dry brush" effect, you can apply a very small amount of paint with the flat of the knife lightly over a fairly dry, flatly painted surface.

The edge of the blade is perfect for lines or edges. Pick up the color and draw it edgewise along the line to be painted. The tip of a pointed knife is good for applying very small areas or dots of color.

Speeding Allowed

The "happy accidents" that so often occur when you paint with a knife will amaze and delight you. See what happens when you put on paint thickly, then scrape it off, put on more paint and scrape again. You can experiment in this way without planning your various applications of paint beforehand. Stop whenever you are pleased with the results! It will be sooner than you think, and your

Oscar Kokoschka's "Self Portrait" (Museum of Modern Art, New York—purchase).

painting will have a warm, mellow look plus a hint of expertness!

You will find new vistas of enjoyment and freedom opening up for you when you paint with a knife. The boldness of the technique and the speed with which you can work allow you to complete a palette knife portrait in one painting session. And at the end, there are no brushes to clean!

When to Use the Knife

Palette knife painting, though a great deal of fun for the artist, does not lend itself well to all portraits. You will not want to paint every portrait with a knife, but if you use discretion in choosing appropriate subjects, you will find the process most rewarding.

If you find a subject you feel can be painted with a knife, by all means do so. It will keep your painting style from becoming too tight and furnish you with a refreshing and stimulating painting experience.

The painting on page 81, executed entirely with a palette knife, was my first attempt. The subject was particularly suitable for this method because of her clear-cut features and broad facial planes.

A Portrait Executed with the Knife

The girl in the painting (page 80) was the model in a life drawing class, but I knew as soon as she started to pose that I had to paint her as well. Her interesting bone structure as well as her sultry, exotic expression interested me extremely. Since she was to pose for one session only, I knew that it would be impossible to complete or even get a good start on an oil painting in class, so I made as many sketches as I could in the two hours, and then I took and developed an instant snapshot.

The combination of sketches, snapshot and the memory of the fascinating model proved sufficient. I spent several hours working up the sketch before I

Studio photograph with an instant-developing camera of the subject from which the painting on the opposite page evolved. Obtaining an accurate likeness with emphasis on the pensive eyes was the aim.

Palette-knife painting made from the photograph opposite.

Photograph used as the basis for the portrait of the young boy.

First stage in painting on the canvas.

Middle stage in painting.

The final portrait.

Final photograph after toy dog was introduced.

First stage in painting the girl.

Middle stage in painting.

The final portrait.

First stage in painting on the canvas.

Second stage in painting the boy with guitar.

Third stage.

The final portrait.

Portrait of an older woman. The straw hat not only frames the face, but gives breadth to the portrait.

Pastel painting in which subtle color effects were achieved.

The object was to show strength of character and preserve the youthfulness of the sitter.

96

Photographing the subject with an instant-developing camera. In the final painting, the colors have to be checked with the live model, because a black-and-white photograph tends to distort color values. For example, the blond hair photographed dark.

started to paint in my studio at home. I chose a straight-forward view, partly because it is the easiest to paint and partly to get the full benefit of her wonderful wide-spread eyes. Then, working with the happy abandon that palette knives engender, I finished the entire portrait in one afternoon.

Putting on the Paint

It is always an exciting moment when you decide which colors you will use in your painting and begin squeezing the tubes on to the palette. Because of the expression of the model and her bold features, a good bright red seemed appropriate for the background. For the flesh I chose burnt sienna, a rich brown; yellow ochre, an almost indispensible color for mixing skin tones, and other earth colors. I chose ultramarine blue, which looks beautiful with cadmium and Venetian reds, and mixes well with both colors, as the cool blue for the painting.

The palette, then, contained the following colors: yellow ochre, cadmium red light, Venetian red, ultra-marine blue, burnt sienna, burnt umber, black, and flake white.

I began the background by using the side of the knife to scrape some cadmium red thinly across the canvas, covering all the background area. Working from dark to light, usually a sound technique, is especially desirable with the palette knife. As you cover the darker colors, which give depth, with lighter colors which advance, you get a natural feeling of creating form as you work.

For the color areas in medium shadow I mixed ultra-marine, burnt sienna, a touch of yellow ochre and white. I applied this mixture rather thickly to the shadowed neck area, across the brow, lower cheeks and the shadow cast by the prominent clavicle bones. I used burnt umber to define the deepest shadows and give a little outline, applying the paint with the edge of the knife. I mixed black and ultramarine and applied it generously with the flat of the knife to the hair area.

The medium and deep skin tones were a mixture of Venetian red, ultramarine, ochre and white, blended at the edges with the shadow colors. To tone down the white for the whites of the eyes I added a bit of yellow ochre.

With most of the skin tones established, it was time to subdue the bright red of the background. I used the flat of my knife to pick up some ultramarine and white and scumble it on the red of the background, letting some of the pure red show through. As I worked, I applied some of this blue and white mixture to small areas of the face to make them recede and to unify the painting. I used a paler, whiter shade of blue in the background just above the shoulders and the dark edges of the face and hair. You can see how this effect of halation, or the overflowing of light, causes the head to stand out from the background.

Finishing Touches

Adding the highlights and definitions is always fun, because they really spark up the painting. To the painter at work, they are like the dessert at the end of the meal, or the pot of gold at the end of the rainbow!

To emphasize the highlights of face and shoulders, I used a combination of yellow ochre and white. I also added a white highlight to each eye, and I outlined the eyes with the tip of the knife, using the mixture of black and ultramarine already applied to the hair. I also outlined the irises, eyebrows, nose and mouth. Now the form of the mouth needed further definition, so I used the highlight color of yellow and white, and a touch of cadmium red here and there on the lips.

A step back. A squint at the painting on the easel. A few touches of paint to redefine the darker areas where needed, and the portrait was finished.

8.

Painting the Portraits of Children

Children have personalities and traits as diverse and interesting as adults. Often their expression changes from moment to moment. The expression and attitude you choose to paint should be the one most characteristic of the child—not one that is rare and fleeting.

Get to Know the Child First

Most children are natural and spontaneous. Some live in a world of their own, inhabited by their own special "visions of sugarplums" while others are as practical and down-to-earth as can be, but all children look most at home in a familiar, natural setting. You can paint a child indoors or out, but choose a setting in which he feels comfortable and secure so that he will really "belong".

Since children are often shy or reticent in the company of strangers, it is a good idea to spend a little extra time winning over your young subject. It is quite easy to get to know most children. Often just showing an interest in what they are doing at the moment and asking a few questions is enough to place them squarely in your corner. A child with an inquiring mind may be interested in hearing how you will go about painting his portrait.

While you are sketching and painting a child it is helpful if you can keep up some sort of a running conversation. It is a rare child who can relax and really sit for you, so don't count on it! Instead, try to remember what you have learned of the child's interests during your preliminary getting-acquainted period, so you can ask questions which will keep him busy and interested in the answering.

Capturing the Expression

Because the attention period of children is limited, their myriad expressions happen quickly and change rapidly. They become bored easily. If you see a child's portrait with an impish or joyful expression, a look of glowing wonder or keen interest, you know the child didn't "hold the pose" for sitting after sitting. The portrait was painted partly from the artist's memory but you can be almost sure the artist used the additional help of a photograph taken at the exact moment!

You may or may not be successful in getting the child to pose for you in a preconceived position and attitude. Probably you will have to take a number of quick snapshots, some posed and some candid, and hope that one will come out the way you want it. Nowhere is an instant-developing camera more useful than in working with children!

Rubens' "Head of a Child" (Liechtenstein Gallery, Vaduz).

Planning the Over-all Picture

The color scheme of a child's portrait requires considerable forethought. A vividly colored canvas may be overpowering, especially if the child's coloring is delicate; a pale, wishy-washy background will drain the subject of animation, while a background that is too dark may seem gloomy and oppressive. To find a happy medium, drench the child in sunlight, without too many deep shadows, or place him in a light-free setting and let him be the focus of attention. Keep the background neutral. An indefinite interior or a rather faint landscape will enhance a child's personality.

Blues and greens are often flattering colors for backgrounds against which to pose a child. You can use them

Murillo's "Peasant Boy"
(National Gallery, London).

for a softly suggested landscape if they seem right for the particular child's coloring, or for a simpler background of interesting brushwork in an abstract manner. In any case, keep the background simple, with the colors greyed and close to each other in value.

You can achieve a lovely effect of light focused on the child, by means of halation. Lighten the background somewhat around the subject's head and darken it gradually towards the outer edges of the canvas. This is especially effective in a simple background of colors without shapes.

Clothing

The same general suggestions which apply to the background are valid for the child's clothing too. The colors can be bright and interesting, but not harsh or competitive. Sharp patterns will seldom work out well. If you must cope with wild prints or plaids or combinations of colors which the child or perhaps his parent insists on, tone them down as you see fit. It is your artistic license to suggest a plaid instead of painting it, to mute colors, to delete extraneous trimmings and to move a pocket, if necessary, to bring the painting into harmony.

If you are consulted as to clothing, hold out for subtle, flattering colors and simplicity of style. We have all seen portraits of little boys in stiff-collared shirts and too-adult suits and wondered what these children were really like in their own milieu. Children's portraits today are free from the restraint which caused former generations to dress their children in their self-conscious Sunday best for portraits. Today casual clothes, and even hard-worn, rumpled playclothes may be your most artistic choice for bringing out the personality of the little imp you are about to paint!

Beginning to Put the Child on Canvas

Once you have taken satisfactory snapshots and perhaps made sketches from life, you can work at your leisure on further studies until you are satisfied. Transfer your sketch to canvas and, if you are planning an underpainting, you are ready to get started on it.

Next you can rough in the flesh tones, the hair, clothing and background in thicker oils. Remember always to have some color on all areas of the canvas, even if the colors change before the final portrait is completed.

Planes of a child's face, from Bridgman.

In painting a child you will notice that there is likely to be very little difference between the deeper color of the shadows and the local color of the skin. Too much contrast will tend to make the child look older. The real

103

contrast in a child's face is found in the eyes, the hair and the bright highlights of the face. If you have started by painting in a general, medium skin tone, you can continue with the cooler shadow tones as well as the warmer highlights.

Keep your areas general and do not attempt too much detail at this stage. However, the painter who is striving for a portrait, as against a painting which makes only a stab at resemblance, will find it helpful to maintain a likeness throughout that painting process. So do not hesitate to put in the general color of the eyes. Delineate the eyebrows which can add so much to the expression of the face, early in the painting, for they will do much to create the likeness. You can put a little color in for the mouth, or suggest the mouth by means of the shadow below the lower lip.

Eastman Johnson's painting of "The Blatchford Brothers" (from a private collection).

104

9.
Painting
the Portraits
of Adults

Painting an adult challenges the artist to portray a feeling of character rather than an expression; a feeling of the kind of life a person has experienced rather than the superficial expression of the moment.

It is usually easier to achieve a likeness of an older person than a young one, for life has left its mark in the form of clear lines upon the face. The bony structure is more evident, for the flesh which clothes it has lost some of its firmness and reveals the contours underlying it. The eyes are usually deeper set, causing sharper shadows. It behooves the artist to paint with restraint and understanding to avoid any touch of caricature.

Capturing the Wisdom of Age

Older people perhaps more than any others should be painted in a sympathetic manner. If the artist does not see beauty in age, his painting will reveal nothing; that is, nothing but the unattractive façade of age.

Your portrait will have real character if you paint it to show stature, repose, wisdom, mellowness, etc. The many interesting qualities inherent in an older person can easily be captured by the observant painter. For instance, if your older subject has a sprightly outlook on life, *paint* it! The sparkle in his eye, contrasting with the somewhat sagging muscles, will make a wonderfully stimulating painting.

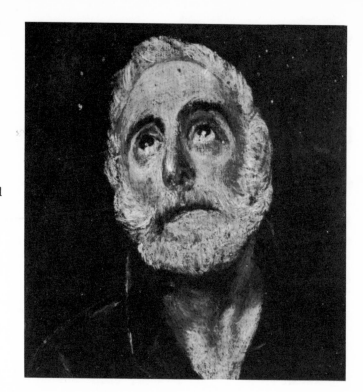

"Saint Peter," detail, by El Greco (National Gallery, London).

Let Your Portrait Age Gracefully!

Painting age in itself is not the object of the portrait painter. Suggesting an aged face is far more interesting than painting every line and hollow. Instead of using dark lines to show the folds of the skin, paint the raised areas of the folds in lighter, warmer tones, and the deeper areas in cooler shadow colors. Use subtle gradations and not harsh lines.

Remember, too, that it is not necessary to paint each and every fold and wrinkle. Begin by painting only those which influence the planes and lend real character to the face. Suggest only as many additional lines as you feel are necessary to make the person look his age—or reasonably close to his years . . .

Bone Structure

If you have studied anatomy and bone structure at all, you will be particularly rewarded for your efforts when it comes to painting older people. The firm flesh of youth which encased the underlying contents has lost its muscle tone, and the softer flesh now reveals the basic bone structure.

The planes of the face change and in a sense exaggerate what was always inherently there. The cheeks tend to become more hollow, even in a well-fleshed face. We have already noted that the eyes have become deeper set. Their muscles, too, have aged and the fatty tissues which formerly supported them from behind have disappeared or lessened. Another change occurs around the mouth because the gums of an older person shrink somewhat and the face tends to fall in above the upper teeth and below the lower. This causes the mouth itself to be more prominent, especially if it were so originally. The eyes of the artist will note these changes, which are among the least flattering aspects of aging, but his heart will probably tell him to minimize their effects!

To suggest the hollows around the cheekbone, use a redder skin color at the edge of the plane. Then place a parallel highlight above or below, depending upon whether the source of light is above or below.

Beware of too much color contrast in the portrait of an older person. Over-dramatizing an aged face may make it look harsh. If a large part of the subject's head is in shadow because of strong side-lighting, that is one thing, but the shadows within a fairly well-lit face should be softer and lighter than usual to obtain a sympathetic rendering.

Posture Tells a Story

The body of the older person suggests age as much as the lines of his face. The composed and relaxed attitude

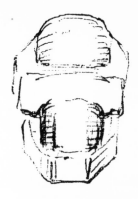

Structure of the face, as shown by Bridgman.

107

of the shoulders and hands reveal the poise one gains with age.

The shoulders are usually round rather than angular, even those of a thin person will have sagged somewhat, bony though they may be, so that clothing will round the contours. If you are painting more than a head, you will probably want to pay special attention to the length of sleeves of dress or coat. The upper arms of an older woman are not one of her most flattering features, and longer sleeves are more becoming.

The hand position will naturally tell its tale of strength, placidity, tenderness, etc. Here too changes have occurred. The veins can be very expressive in an older man, but unflattering in a woman. Paint them as raised areas with cool shadows, as in the lines of the face. The joints of the fingers tend to become enlarged in older people, or at least they look more pronounced because the flesh has shrunk a bit. They look less graceful than those of a younger person, but nevertheless they have their own beauty which you can suggest by blurring all the outlines somewhat.

Painting Grey Hair

Grey hair is not difficult to paint. If it is a thick head of hair, it will appear darker near the scalp because the roots are in considerable shadow. If, however, the subject has fine silvery hair which has grown thin, much pink scalp will show through, even in the painting of a woman. In either case, paint in the darker tones first and then you can scumble in the lighter tones effectively.

Squint at your subject and note how many different colors you see in the hair, reflected from the scalp itself and from the surroundings. The grey hair itself shows a variety of shades and colors, but you should not go into detail nor attempt to paint each hair, the dark along with the white and grey. Squint again and try to see the hair in areas of warmer and cooler greys, and paint it in areas

"La Vieille au Chapelet" by Cézanne (National Gallery, London).

to obtain the effect you are seeking. Burnt umber and a blue are good pigments to mix in as you paint white hair. Experiment, too, with black and terre verte.

Do not emphasize the bald head of an older man unless he has a particularly handsome and imposing skull. Avoid the temptation to paint shiny highlights, and use a subtle gradation of color to show form.

Thomas Eakins' "Portrait of Walt Whitman" (Pennsylvania Academy of the Fine Arts, Philadelphia).

Eyes and Eyeglasses

The eyes of an older person are almost always his most thought-provoking feature. The viewer cannot help being aware of all that those eyes have seen!

Paint an older subject in a flattering manner with slightly uplifted eyes . . . like a lovely old tree gently reaching for the sky. The eyes should appear soft, with the iris blending in a liquid manner into the white of the eyeball. To get this effect in paint, blend the outer edges of the iris (Renoir did this sort of blending with the wooden tip of the wrong end of his brush) into the white of the eye, but grey the white more than you would for a younger person. The eyes of older people are deeper set and therefore more shadowed altogether, whites as well as lids.

There is generally more than one fold in the upper eyelid of an elderly person. The folds may not parallel each other, but may break in divers directions. Suggest but do not overemphasize these highly characteristic lines and shadows.

You can create a twinkle in the eye by curving upwards the line at the outer edge of one or both eyelids. Note carefully where to place the highlight on the eyelid to accentuate the effect of the twinkle.

If your subject is wearing glasses, paint the eyes as you normally would, disregarding the glasses. You may want to ask your subject to leave his glasses off while you are at this stage of the painting. Then paint a partial outline of the glasses and some light reflections on the lenses in a light color.

Wistful, poignant, jovial, resigned—the character your subject has gained over the years will be a rewarding challenge to you, the portraitist.

INDEX